DANGEROUS ADVENTURES

Airplane Adventures

by Karen and Glen Bledsoe

Consultants:
Mike Jackson, Lt. Col., USAF (Ret)
Executive Director
National Aviation Hall of Fame

Tara Engel
Historian
National Aviation Hall of Fame

CAPSTONE
HIGH-INTEREST

Capstone High-Interest Books are published by Capstone Press
151 Good Counsel Drive, P.O. Box 669, Mankato, Minnesota 56002
http://www.capstone-press.com

Library of Congress Cataloging-in-Publication Data
Bledsoe, Karen E.
    Airplane adventures/by Karen and Glen Bledsoe.
    p. cm.—(Dangerous adventures)
    Includes bibliographical references and index.
    ISBN 0-7368-0903-1
    1. Aeronautics—Records—Juvenile literature. [1. Aeronautics—History.]
I. Bledsoe, Glen. II. Title. III. Series.
TL537 .B58 2002
629.13'009—dc21   00-012527

Summary: Describes adventures in flying airplanes, including a history of the first
airplanes, adventures of early pilots, and current airplane adventures.

Editorial Credits
Tom Adamson, editor; Lois Wallentine, product planning editor; Heather Kindseth,
    cover designer; Timothy Halldin, production designer and illustrator; Katy Kudela,
    photo researcher

Photo Credits
AFFTC History Office, 10
American Stock/Archive Photos, 14
Archive Photos, 9, 16, 20, 24, 26, 30, 32
Courtesy of Amer Khashoggi, 40
Courtesy of Tom Claytor, 38
Doug Shane/Courtesy of Jeana Yeager, 34
Graeme Teague, 6
Photo Network/Mark Newman, cover
Photri-Microstock, 4
Smithsonian Institution Archives, 12, 18
Wright Re-creations, 42

Table of Contents

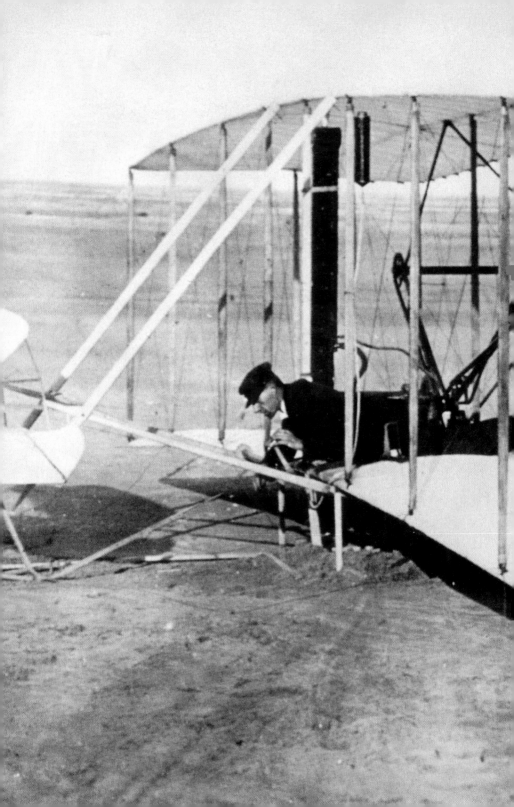

Chapter 1

Airplane Adventures

On December 17, 1903, Orville and Wilbur Wright stood on a beach near Kitty Hawk, North Carolina. Orville climbed into the airplane that the two brothers had built. The machine was made mostly of wood, wire, and canvas. It was named the *Wright Flyer*.

The Wright brothers started the gasoline engine that turned the propellers. The *Flyer* moved forward. Orville pulled back on the control stick. The *Flyer* rose into the air and flew 120 feet (37 meters). At that moment, Orville became the first person to fly a powered airplane.

On December 17, 1903, the Wright brothers became the first people to fly a powered airplane.

Some small airplanes have propellers.

Eighty-three years later, Dick Rutan and Jeana Yeager stepped into their airplane, the *Voyager*. It was made of special lightweight plastics. Rutan and Yeager flew the *Voyager* around the world in nine days. They did not stop, even for fuel. It was the first nonstop, unrefueled airplane flight around the world. The *Voyager* had flown 24,986 miles (40,210 kilometers).

How Airplanes Work

Some airplanes have propellers. Propellers are shaped like small wings. They usually are located at the nose of the airplane. A gasoline engine turns the propeller. This rotation helps pull the plane through the air.

Many airplanes have jet engines instead of rotating propellers. Jet engines pull in air. The air presses together tightly. The compressed air mixes with high-energy fuel. This mixture burns inside the engine and creates hot gases. These gases are forced out the back of the engine. The force of the gases pushes the plane forward. Jet airplanes usually are faster than propeller-driven airplanes.

Most airplanes have fixed wings. The front edges of these stiff wings are curved. The tops of the wings also are curved. This curved shape causes air to speed up as it flows over the wing. The air creates low pressure across the top of the wing. Slower-moving air under the wing creates high pressure. The difference in air pressures creates lift. Lift allows the airplane to fly.

Airplane wings have ailerons. These devices are at the trailing edges of the wings. Ailerons help turn a plane.

Some wings also have flaps. Flaps can turn downward to lengthen the trailing edge of the wing. The flaps help lift the airplane during takeoffs. Flaps also help to slow down the plane during landings. They turn farther downward to slow the plane's speed.

Adventurers in the Air

The first people to fly airplanes faced many dangers. Many pilots had little flight training. Some pilots taught themselves to fly. Pilots took off from and landed in rough fields instead of on smooth runways. Early airplanes were easily damaged by high winds and rough landings. These planes also had open cockpits that provided no protection for pilots. Many early pilots died in crashes or by falling from the cockpit during flight.

Pilots often followed roads or railroad tracks to find their way. They used hand-held

Early airplanes were made of canvas, wood, and wire. These planes had no cockpits.

compasses to find the direction they were traveling. Some early pilots used a carpenter's level to see if the plane was level or tilting. This tool has a tube of liquid with a bubble of air. As a plane tilted, the bubble of air moved.

Many people enjoyed flying despite the dangers. Early pilots wanted adventure.

Modern Improvements

Over the years, airplane design improved. Airplanes were built with closed cockpits to protect pilots. Airplanes could fly longer distances and carry heavier loads. New instruments helped pilots control and navigate their planes.

Today, commercial airliners fly all around the world. Military planes fly many times faster than the speed of sound. People who want to fly today must take lessons and earn a pilot's license. They spend many hours practicing with experienced pilots. Pilots have set many flying records. But flying is still an adventure.

Today, military planes can fly faster than the speed of sound.

Chapter 2

Famous Firsts

In the late 1800s, inventors tried to build flying machines. Some early machines had wings that flapped like bird wings. Some had fixed wings. None of these machines flew.

The First Airplane Flight

Samuel P. Langley was a famous scholar at the Smithsonian Institution. He experimented with airplanes.

In October 1903, Langley invited reporters to watch Charles Manly fly over the Potomac River in Washington, D.C. Langley's plane fell into the river. Manly and Langley tried a second time. But they could not get the plane in the air. Many newspaper reporters wrote that powered flight was impossible.

Langley's attempted airplane flight in 1903 failed.

Orville Wright became the first person to fly an airplane.

Orville and Wilbur Wright had been experimenting with gliders. These winged aircraft have no propellers or engines. The Wrights put a gasoline engine on one of their gliders. The engine turned two propellers. These propellers pushed the craft through the air.

On December 17, 1903, they tested the *Flyer* on a beach near Kitty Hawk, North Carolina. The *Flyer* flew 120 feet (37 meters) on its first run that day. The brothers took turns flying the plane. On its fourth flight, Wilbur flew the airplane 852 feet (260 meters).

The Wrights told the newspapers what they had done. But few newspapers printed the story. Few people believed that two unknown brothers could succeed while Langley had failed.

Crossing the English Channel

In 1909, an English newspaper offered a prize to the first pilot who could fly across the English Channel. This body of water separates England from France. The prize was 1,000 pounds. This amount was about $5,000 in U.S. money at the time.

Louis Blériot built airplanes in France. He experimented with monoplanes. These planes have a single large wing on each side of the fuselage. Blériot and another French pilot named Hubert Latham accepted the challenge.

Both men took their planes to a beach near Calais, France. Latham took off in his monoplane on the morning of July 19. His engine quit before he was halfway across. The plane fell into the water.

In 1909, Louis Blériot became the first person to fly across the English Channel.

Latham waited for his plane to be repaired. He sent friends to watch Blériot. Latham did not want Blériot to get a head start.

Blériot made several test flights of his *Blériot XI* monoplane. On July 25, Blériot took off early in the morning. Latham's friends thought that it was another test flight. But Blériot then headed toward the channel. Latham's friends ran to tell him. Blériot was gone before Latham could rush to his plane.

Blériot flew into a strong wind. He had no windshield to protect him. He continued flying steadily. Soon he could see the white cliffs of Dover, England. His friend Charles Fontaine stood on top of a cliff waving a French flag. Blériot landed on top of the cliffs. His flight lasted 37 minutes and was about 24 miles (39 kilometers) in length. Blériot was the first person to fly across the English Channel.

Across the United States

On October 10, 1910, U.S. newspaper publisher William Randolph Hearst started a contest. Hearst offered $50,000 to the first pilot who could fly across the United States in 30 days or fewer. The offer was good for one year.

Cal Rodgers accepted Hearst's challenge. Rodgers learned to fly at the Wright brothers' flying school. Rodgers asked the Wright brothers to design a biplane for him. A company that made a grape-flavored soft drink called Vin Fiz sponsored the flight.

Rodgers named his plane the *Vin Fiz*. It could fly for three and one-half hours on 15 gallons (57 liters) of gasoline. Rodgers would be able to

Cal Rodgers took off from New York City on his flight across the United States.

fly about 150 miles (240 kilometers) at a time. He would have to fly in the daytime because he did not have lights or navigation instruments. A train carrying spare parts, his crew, and his family would travel along his flight path. Rodgers planned to follow the train as he flew.

Rodgers took off from New York City on September 17, 1911. He flew 84 miles (135 kilometers) the first day. He landed safely in Middletown, New York. The next day, he struck a tree on takeoff and crashed into a chicken coop. His crew needed three days to repair the plane.

The rest of the flight continued in the same way. Rodgers crashed 16 times during his trip. Five of the crashes were so serious that the plane had to be rebuilt. His crew estimated that they could have built four planes from the parts used to repair the *Vin Fiz*.

On October 10, Rodgers had only reached Marshall, Missouri. The time limit had expired. Rodgers continued his journey even though he knew he could not collect Hearst's prize. On November 5, he landed the *Vin Fiz* in Pasadena, California. The trip took 49 days. Rodgers wanted to continue flying to the Pacific Ocean. But he crashed again and broke his ankle.

Rodgers rebuilt the plane after a month of recovery. He flew it to Long Beach, California. Rodgers rolled the plane across a beach until the wheels touched the ocean. His journey from New York had taken 84 days.

Chapter 3

Long-Distance Flights

Many countries worked to improve airplane design. Their military engineers built larger aircraft. They made the engines more powerful. They improved and added instruments. These changes helped make long-distance flying possible.

During World War I (1914–1918), the British military built the Vickers Vimy bomber. This plane was never used because the war ended before the plane was ready.

Nonstop across the Atlantic

Two English pilots were the first to fly across the Atlantic Ocean nonstop. The pilots were

Alcock and Brown were the first pilots to fly nonstop across the Atlantic Ocean.

TIMELINE

1900s–1910s

1903
The Wright brothers fly the *Wright Flyer*, the first powered airplane.

1908
Thomas Selfridge dies in a plane crash in Virginia. He becomes the first airplane fatality.

1909
Louis Blériot becomes the first person to fly across the English Channel.

1911
Cal Rodgers flies across the United States in the *Vin Fiz*.

1912
Harriet Quimby becomes the first woman to fly solo across the English Channel.

1920s

1919
John Alcock and Arthur Whitten-Brown complete the first nonstop flight across the Atlantic Ocean.

1923
Oakley Kelly and John Macready complete the first nonstop flight across the United States.

1927
Charles Lindbergh flies the *Spirit of St. Louis* nonstop from New York City to Paris to make the first solo transatlantic flight.

1930s–1950s

1932
Amelia Earhart becomes the first woman to fly solo across the Atlantic Ocean.

1933
Wiley Post flies solo around the world in 7 days, 18 hours, and 49 minutes.

1947
Chuck Yeager pilots the first aircraft to break the sound barrier.

1957
Jacqueline Cochran becomes the first female pilot to fly faster than the speed of sound.

1980s–present

1986
Dick Rutan and Jeana Yeager fly the *Voyager* around the world nonstop and without refueling.

1994
Fred Lasby becomes the oldest person to fly around the world at age 82.

2000
Chris Wall and Dan Dominguez become the youngest pilots to fly around the world.

John Alcock and Arthur Whitten-Brown. The pilots converted a Vickers Vimy bomber into a plane that could fly long distances. They added extra fuel tanks. They removed all of the plane's bombing equipment.

On June 14, 1919, Alcock and Brown took off from Newfoundland, Canada. They planned to fly to Ireland. The distance was 1,880 miles (3,025 kilometers).

The pilots flew into a storm over the Atlantic. Alcock tried to fly above the storm. But the engine stalled. The plane went into a spin. Alcock pulled the plane out of the spin only 50 feet (15 meters) above the water.

On the morning of July 15, the two men finally saw the coast of Ireland. Alcock flew the Vimy to an area that looked like a field. The flat area was actually a soft bog. The wheels stuck in the soft, wet ground. The plane tipped up on its nose. Alcock and Brown were not hurt. Their trip lasted about 16 hours.

Another Atlantic Challenge

In 1919, hotel manager Raymond Orteig offered $25,000 to the first person who could

Charles Lindbergh flew the *Spirit of St. Louis* alone across the Atlantic Ocean in 1927.

fly nonstop between New York and Paris. The trip's distance is 3,600 miles (5,800 kilometers). Most pilots thought that the risks were too great. No one accepted the challenge for several years.

Charles Lindbergh accepted Orteig's challenge in May 1927. Lindbergh knew that the flight would be dangerous. He would be alone. There would be no one to take turns flying with him.

Lindbergh's plane was called the *Spirit of St. Louis*. Lindbergh modified the plane for the flight. The plane had to be as lightweight as possible. It would need to carry enough fuel for the trip. It had no radio, instruments, or even a parachute. The plane's only navigation instrument was a compass. To see forward, Lindbergh had to look through a homemade periscope. This tube-shaped device had mirrors that reflected what was in front of the plane.

When Lindbergh arrived in New York, several other pilots already were there. They hoped to win Orteig's prize. They were waiting for the weather to clear. Four pilots already had taken off and had crashed. Two of the pilots died.

Lindbergh's Flight

Lindbergh prepared the *Spirit of St. Louis* to leave on May 20, 1927. His crew filled the tanks with 451 gallons (1,707 liters) of fuel. Lindbergh put five sandwiches, two canteens

Amelia Earhart flew alone across the Atlantic Ocean in 1932.

of water, and a thermos of coffee in his cockpit. He used a map and a compass to stay on course.

Lindbergh took off at 7:52 in the morning. The extra fuel made the plane heavy. Lindbergh barely cleared the telephone lines at the end of the runway.

In the middle of the night, Lindbergh noticed that the plane was not flying properly.

He reached out the window and felt ice. With his flashlight, he saw that the plane was coated with ice. He knew that ice would interfere with the plane's ability to fly. He flew at a lower altitude until he found warmer air. The ice soon melted.

Lindbergh finally spotted land in the afternoon of the flight's second day. He checked his map. He was approaching Ireland.

When Lindbergh reached Paris, he flew around the Eiffel Tower. He then landed at Le Bourget Airfield on May 21, 1927. The flight lasted 33 and one-half hours.

First Woman across the Atlantic
In 1928, Amy Guest decided that a woman should fly across the Atlantic. Guest bought a Fokker monoplane called the *Friendship*. She hired two men to fly the plane. Wilmer Stultz was an expert pilot. Lou Gordon was a flight mechanic. Guest then chose pilot Amelia Earhart to fly with them. Earhart had set a women's altitude record in 1922. She had flown 14,000 feet (4,300 meters) into the air.

On June 17, the *Friendship* took off from Trepassey, Newfoundland, and headed for Ireland. The crew flew into fog several hours into the flight. The radio quit working. The *Friendship* could not radio for directions. The airplane continued through the fog.

The *Friendship* was almost out of fuel when the crew saw land. They landed in a bay near a fishing village. They had flown past Ireland and had landed in Burry Port, Wales.

Earhart became famous for being the first woman to fly across the Atlantic. But she did not feel that she deserved the fame. She did not actually fly the plane.

In 1932, Earhart planned to fly across the Atlantic by herself. She bought a Lockheed Vega monoplane. On May 20, 1932, Earhart took off from Newfoundland. She flew alone through fog and clouds. She reached Ireland the next day and landed the Vega in a cow pasture. She was the first woman to fly a plane solo across the Atlantic.

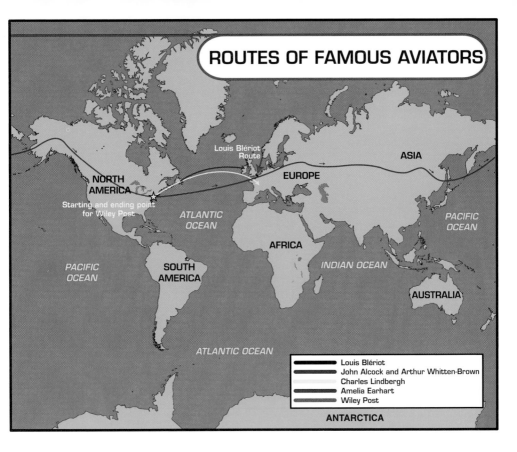

ROUTES OF FAMOUS AVIATORS

Louis Blériot
Route

ASIA

NORTH
AMERICA

EUROPE

Starting and ending point
for Wiley Post

ATLANTIC
OCEAN

PACIFIC
OCEAN

AFRICA

PACIFIC
OCEAN

SOUTH
AMERICA

INDIAN OCEAN

AUSTRALIA

ATLANTIC OCEAN

Louis Blériot
John Alcock and Arthur Whitten-Brown
Charles Lindbergh
Amelia Earhart
Wiley Post

ANTARCTICA

Wiley Post

In 1931, Wiley Post set a record for flying
around the world. He chose Harold Gatty as
his navigator. His airplane was a Lockheed
Vega called the *Winnie Mae*. Post and Gatty
replaced the passenger seats with fuel tanks.

Post and Gatty took off from New York on
June 23, 1931. They flew across the Atlantic to
Europe. They continued flying across Asia. The

Wiley Post flew the *Winnie Mae* alone around the world in 1933.

pilots turned north to avoid flying over the Pacific. They crossed the Bering Sea and flew south across Alaska. They continued east across Canada. Post and Gatty landed in New York on July 1. They made 13 stops to refuel along the way. Their trip had taken 8 days, 15 hours, and 51 minutes.

On July 15, 1933, Post took off alone from New York in the *Winnie Mae*. He flew almost the same path that he and Gatty had flown before. Post used an early autopilot device. The device helped him stay on course.

Post flew to Berlin, Germany, without stopping. He then continued across Asia. A few days later, he reached Alaska. There, he bent his propeller while landing. Mechanics repaired it quickly. Post continued on to Edmonton, Canada. He arrived back in New York on July 22, 1933. Post had set a new record of 7 days, 18 hours, and 49 minutes. He was also the first person to fly solo around the world.

Chapter 4

Farther and Faster

Airplanes became more important to the
military during World War II (1939–1945).
Planes became larger and faster. They could
fly longer distances and carry heavier loads.
After the war, pilots began trying for new
flight records.

"The Fastest Man Alive"

The U.S. Air Force experimented with new
rocket engines near the end of World War II.
Engineers tested an experimental rocket-powered
airplane called the Bell X-1. Captain Chuck
Yeager was chosen to pilot the plane.

On October 14, 1947, a large bomber plane
carried the Bell X-1 into the air. The plane was
attached to the bottom of the bomber. The Bell

Chuck Yeager was called "the fastest man alive" after
he broke the sound barrier.

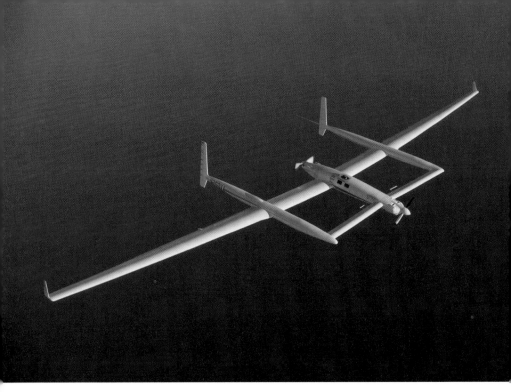

Voyager's lightweight design allowed the plane to carry enough fuel to travel around the world without stopping.

X-1 was launched in mid-air. Yeager flew the Bell X-1 at the speed of sound. The speed of sound is called Mach 1. This speed is about 760 miles (1,223 kilometers) per hour at sea level. At an altitude of 40,000 feet (12,200 meters), the speed of sound is about 660 miles (1,060 kilometers) per hour. Yeager was the first person ever to fly at this speed.

In December 1953, Yeager flew another rocket-powered plane called the Bell X-1A.

This plane could travel at more than twice the speed of sound. As he reached Mach 2.5, Yeager lost control of the craft. It tumbled end over end. Yeager regained control and landed safely. Newspapers called him "the fastest man alive."

Voyager

In 1986, Dick Rutan and Jeana Yeager became the first pilots to fly around the world nonstop and without refueling. They flew a special aircraft made of lightweight plastics. They called their plane the *Voyager*.

The *Voyager* carried its fuel in its wings. The *Voyager*'s long plastic wings were flexible. They bent when the fuel tanks were filled. The plane's designers had to make wings that would provide lift even when bent.

The *Voyager* had two engines. Each engine turned a propeller. One propeller was in front. It pulled the plane through the air. The other engine was in the rear to push the plane. The *Voyager*'s cabin was only 7.5 feet (2.3 meters) long and 4 feet (1.2 meters) wide.

The Flight of the *Voyager*

The *Voyager* began its around-the-world flight on December 14, 1986. Rutan and Yeager took off from Edwards Air Force Base in California. The tanks held 1,207 gallons (4,569 liters) of fuel. The flexible wings were so heavy that they scraped the runway as the plane took off.

The *Voyager* headed out over the Pacific Ocean. The plane passed over Hilo, Hawaii, late on the first day. The *Voyager* reached Africa on the sixth day of the flight. The *Voyager* crossed the Atlantic Ocean on the seventh and eighth days of the flight.

Over the Atlantic Ocean, the pilots flew into a storm. Strong winds tipped the plane sharply. It nearly flipped over. Rutan guided the plane carefully and recovered. But the effort greatly tired Rutan. He could not think clearly. Yeager had to convince him to trade places with her.

On the ninth day, both of the *Voyager*'s engines stopped working. Rutan held the plane steady while Yeager helped restart the engines.

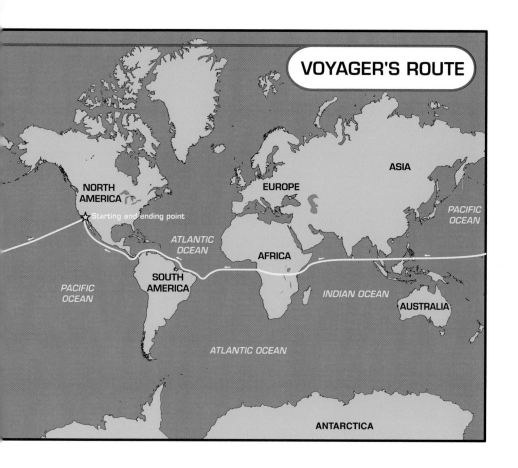

They had dropped to 3,500 feet (1,067 meters) before the front engine started. They then restarted the rear engine.

On December 23, 1986, the *Voyager* reached Edwards Air Force Base. Only 18.3 gallons (69.3 liters) of fuel remained in the tanks when it landed.

Chapter 5

Airplane Adventures Today

Many people have dreamed of creating or breaking a record in an airplane. Plenty of challenges remain for adventurous pilots.

Solo Flight to Every Continent

In December 1990, pilot Tom Claytor took off from Philadelphia, Pennsylvania. He still has not returned home. Claytor hopes to visit every country and all seven continents before he returns. He would become the first solo pilot to do so.

Since 1997, Claytor has visited many countries in the Middle East and Asia. His trip home will include nations in the South Pacific and in South America.

Tom Claytor plans to fly to every country and all seven continents.

Amer Khashoggi believes he and his crew will fly more than 125,000 miles (200,000 kilometers) on their trip.

Youngest to Fly around the World

In 2000, Chris Wall and Dan Dominguez were 21 years old. They became the youngest pilots to fly around the world. Both pilots had been flying since they were teenagers.

Wall and Dominguez flew a small twin-engine Aero Commander 560E airplane named *Dreamcatcher*. Wall rebuilt the 40-year-old plane. He added extra fuel tanks and new instruments.

Wall and Dominguez called their adventure World Flight 2000. *Dreamcatcher* had a video camera and computer. The pilots sent pictures and messages to an Internet site. The pilots left Rochester, New York, on September 13, 2000. They returned to Rochester on December 15.

Fastest Flight to Every Country

Pilot Amer Khashoggi believes there are records to be set for around-the-world flights. He is planning a flight that will include 198 countries and all seven continents.

His trip will be much faster than Claytor's. He believes that it will take his crew of five about five months to complete the journey. The crew will fly a Cessna Grand Caravan 208B. Khashoggi's achievement will be different from Claytor's solo record because he will have a crew.

Smith and Whiting plan to fly two _Vin Fiz_ replicas across the United States.

Re-creating Historical Flights
In 2002, Dana Smith and Ken Whiting plan to duplicate an old record. They will re-create the 1911 coast-to-coast flight of the _Vin Fiz_. They are making this trip to celebrate 100 years of flight.

Smith and Whiting have been building two planes exactly like the one flown by Cal Rodgers. They have studied maps of Rodgers' journey. But they will not follow the exact route. Many of the places where Rodgers landed are now shopping malls and homes. Smith and Whiting's route will closely follow the original. They also will stop at many places where Rodgers did not stop. They want as many people as possible to see their *Vin Fiz* replicas.

Words To Know

autopilot (AW-toh-pye-luht)—a device that helps control the movements of an airplane

cockpit (KOK-pit)—the place near the front of an airplane where the pilot sits

fuselage (FYOO-suh-lahzh)—the main body of an airplane

glider (GLYE-dur)—a winged aircraft that does not have an engine; a glider flies by floating and rising on air currents.

Mach 1 (MAHK WUHN)—a unit for measuring an airplane's speed; Mach 1 is the speed of sound; the speed of sound is about 760 miles (1,223 kilometers) per hour at sea level.

navigate (NAV-uh-gate)—traveling in an airplane using instruments to help guide the plane

propeller (pruh-PEL-ur)—a set of rotating blades that provide the force to move an airplane through the air

44

To Learn More

Burkett, Molly. *Pioneers of the Air.* Great Explorers. Hauppauge, N.Y.: Barron's Educational Series, 1998.

Freedman, Russell. *The Wright Brothers: How They Invented the Airplane.* New York: Holiday House, 1991.

Kent, Zachary. *Charles Lindbergh and the Spirit of St. Louis in American History.* Berkeley Heights, N.J.: Enslow, 2001.

McLoone, Margo. *Women Explorers of the Air.* Capstone Short Biographies. Mankato, Minn.: Capstone High-Interest Books, 2000.

Stein, R. Conrad. *Chuck Yeager Breaks the Sound Barrier.* Cornerstones of Freedom. New York: Children's Press, 1997.

Useful Addresses

American Aviation Historical Society
2333 Otis Street
Santa Ana, CA 92704

National Aviation Hall of Fame
P.O. Box 31096
Dayton, OH 45437

**Smithsonian National Air and Space
  Museum**
Seventh and Independence Avenue SW
Washington, DC 20560

**Wright Brothers Aeroplane Company and
  Museum of Pioneer Aviation**
P.O. Box 204
West Milton, OH 45383

Internet Sites

Aerofiles: American Aviation from 1903 to 2003
http://www.aerofiles.com

NAJACO World Flight
http://najaco.com

National Aviation Hall of Fame
http://www.nationalaviation.org

Smithsonian National Air and Space Museum
http://www.nasm.edu

World Flight 2000
http://worldflight2000.org

Wright Brothers Aeroplane Company and Museum of Pioneer Aviation
http://www.first-to-fly.com

Index